EXTRAORDINARY
TEXAS WOMEN

EXTRAORDINARY TEXAS WOMEN

BY JUDY ALTER

TCU PRESS · FORT WORTH
A TEXAS SMALL BOOK ★

A Texas Small Book
Copyright © 2008 Judy Alter

Library of Congress Cataloging-in-Publication Data

Alter, Judy, 1938-
Extraordinary Texas women / by Judy Alter.
p. cm.
ISBN 978-0-87565-366-2 (alk. paper)
1. Women--Texas--Biography. 2. Texas--Biography.
I. Title.

CT3262.T4A45 2008
920.7209764--dc22

2007033213

TCU Press • P. O. Box 298300 • Fort Worth, TX 76129
817.257.7822

To order books: 800.826.8911
http://www.prs.tcu.edu

Design/Margie Adkins Graphic Design

DEDICATION

To Barbara, Betty, Carol, Elizabeth, Fran, Gayla, Georgia, Jan, Jean, Jeannie, June, Kathie, Kathy, Katie, Linda, Margaret, Margie, Mary, Mary Lu, Melinda, Sheila, Sue, Susan, and all the other extraordinary Texas women of today, who so far remain unsung. And to Megan, Jordan, Melanie, Lisa, Madison, Eden, and Morgan. ★

CONTENTS

EXTRAORDINARY TEXAS WOMEN
AN INTRODUCTION

TEXAS JUST MAY BE THE state in the Union with the strongest masculine image. Our heroes, from cowboys to the Alamo to Stephen F. Austin and Sam Houston, have always been men. But Texas has had some important women, and the state has been good about recognizing some of them, less responsive about others.

The Texans in these pages have made history in a variety of ways—some outrageous, some inventive, most courageous. They have been crusaders, sports stars, entrepreneurs and business leaders, ranchers and cowgirls, philanthropists, artists—and often, characters. For some, their greatest accomplishments and most unusual adventures came after they left Texas, but they are still bound to and influenced by a Texas heritage.

1

These women generally lived outside convention and caught public attention to one degree or another. Countless other women have untold stories that you should also know—women who walked behind a plow, picked cotton, raised a family in a dugout, women who left little record of their lives.

There were, of course, Hispanic and Native American women here long before Jane Long camped on the shores of Galveston Bay. Many minority women of great accomplishment during the nineteenth and twentieth centuries have been left out of the record of Texas history, and their stories need to be told. But their stories are for another book.

Many will disagree with my choices, claiming this woman or that should have been included. I plead that a small book imposes limitations, and, at best, this is but a sampling, an introduction to Texas women, an invitation to explore more deeply. A list of suggested readings offers places to begin your exploration. If you begin with the extraordinary women here and find them interesting, you may move on to the ordinary women who were each in her own way extraordinary.

Why do we read about women of the past? It's an old saw, but knowing the past helps us live in the present. And these women give us role models for the future in their strength and self-confidence. I want my daughters and granddaughters to know about these women—and I hope you do too! ★

An Early Settler

Jane Long

THE TROUBLE WITH TELLING the stories of Texas women of the past is that it's hard to separate fact from folklore. There are no documented sources for much of what we know, only stories handed down from generation to generation. Such is the case with Jane Long, the "Mother of Texas." What we know about Long is based on stories she herself told to Mirabeau B. Lamar (later the second president of Texas) when he toured the state, collecting material for a history that he never wrote.

Long claimed to be the first English-speaking woman to give birth to a child in Texas. But statistics show that simply wasn't true. Nonetheless, she is known as the "Mother of Texas" because of that claim. Her other adventures, trials, and tribulations are worth recounting however.

She was born Jane Wilkinson in 1798 in Maryland. Her father died, and her mother moved to the Mississippi Territory. Jane was still a young teenager when her mother also died. And she wasn't much older when she met James Long, a surgeon in the Battle of New Orleans (War of 1812, between England and the United States). They met in 1815, married in May, and had their first child in November. The couple lived in Natchez for a few years, but in 1819 he left for Nacogdoches in the

Mexican province then known as Tejas. She remained behind with her daughter Ann, and shortly after James' departure, Jane gave birth to Rebecca. Little Rebecca died soon after birth, but Jane and Ann and a twelve-year-old servant named Kian later joined James Long at Bolivar Point on Galveston Bay. He had established Fort Las Casas to assist in the effort to free Texas from Mexican control.

In September 1821, her husband left for a trip to La Bahía but was captured at San Antonio, taken to Mexico City, and "accidentally" killed. Not knowing what had happened to him, Long vowed to remain on Bolivar Point until he returned. As supplies dwindled, other families left. Although she was pregnant again, Long remained behind. She kept Indians away by making the fort appear still occupied, and she survived on corn meal, salted fish, and oysters she harvested from the bay. In December 1821, alone with Kian and Ann in an ice-covered tent—or so the story goes—she gave birth to her third daughter, Mary James. By the summer of 1822 she moved up the Sabine River, still waiting for her husband, when she finally received word that he had been killed.

In 1824 Stephen F. Austin granted Long a league (4500 acres) of land in Fort Bend County and a labor (200 acres) of land in Waller County. Instead of living on her land, she moved to San Felipe and then to Mississippi, where she could put Ann in school.

In 1837, she moved to her property in Fort Bend County, now in the town of Richmond, and opened a boardinghouse. She also developed a plantation south of the town, bought and sold land, raised cattle, and grew cotton (with the help of twelve slaves). Her plantation was valued at about $10,000 in 1840 and her holdings continued to increase. But as she grew older, she was unable to manage her affairs, and she died at the home of a grandson, with her estate valued at only $2,000.

Family legend and folklore claim that Long was courted by some of the leading men of the Texas Republic—Sam Houston, Ben Milam, and Mirabeau B. Lamar. She rejected them all and died in 1880, the widow of James Long.

In 1936 a centennial marker was erected in her honor at Fort Bend County. ★

Jane Long. *Courtesy Texas State Library and Archives Commission.*

WOMEN OF THE TEXAS REVOLUTION

The Texas Revolution brought out some interesting women, not all of them exactly heroines. And we have to read their stories with a skeptical eye, for often the stories are more folklore and myth than they are truth. ★

CAT JENNINGS

FOR INSTANCE, THERE was fourteen-year-old Catherine Jennings of Bastrop, whose father was the oldest Anglo to die at the Alamo. When she heard the news of the fall of the Alamo, with no survivors, she is said to have mounted her horse and ridden across Austin's Colony, urging men to join Sam Houston's ragged army. Her great-great-great granddaughter swears it's true, but she can't find the newspaper clipping about the ride that she once had. Who knows? But it makes a great story. ★

Catherine Jennings. *Drawing by Barbara Whitehead.*
From the cover of *Sam Houston Is My Hero* by
Judy Alter (TCU Press 2003).

Susanna Wilkerson Dickinson

We aren't even sure how to spell her name—sometimes it's Susan, Susana, or Suzanna, and sometimes her maiden name is Wilkinson, sometimes Wilkerson. But Susanna Dickinson has earned her place in Texas history because she and her daughter were supposedly the only Anglo survivors of the massacre at the Alamo. Other women in the Alamo were probably Hispanic.

She married Almaron Dickinson in Tennessee when she was fifteen or sixteen. In 1830 they traveled from Tennessee to Texas, settling in Gonzales. A daughter, Angelina, was born to the Dickinsons in 1834.

In 1831, the Mexican government gave settlers at Gonzales a small cannon for protection against Indian attacks—the settlement had been abandoned in 1826 after two attacks and rebuilt in 1827.

As hostility increased between Texians (a term used to describe citizens of the Anglo-American section of the province of Coahuila and Tejas or of the Republic of Texas) and the government of Mexico, a contingent of Mexican soldiers was sent from San Antonio to retrieve the cannon, but they were met by a band of Texians who had made a banner reading, "Come and take it." The Texians resisted the Federales in the Battle of Gonzales, the first skirmish of the Texas Revolution.

Susanna Wilkerson Dickinson.
Courtesy Texas State Library and Archives Commission.

When thirty-two men from Gonzales marched off to defend the Alamo, Almaron Dickinson was among them. His wife stayed behind until Mexican troops looted her home. Then she took her daughter to San Antonio, staying briefly at the home of an acquaintance. In late February, she and Angelina moved into the Alamo.

After the battle Mexican soldiers took her and the other women and children to the same home where she had stayed. Santa Anna came to talk privately to each of them, gave each a blanket and two dollars in silver, and sent them on their way. He gave Dickinson a letter to Sam Houston, who was by then at Gonzales, organizing his army. She brought Houston the first news of the massacre, and he immediately had Gonzales burned and ordered a retreat.

Thus began the Runaway Scrape, where Houston marched his troops east across Texas, joined by terrified citizens fleeing the advancing Mexican army. Dickinson no doubt went with the other widows of Gonzales on the march.

The rest of her story is not quite so heroic. She married and divorced, one of the first divorces in Harris County. She married again three more times, and there are rumors that she lived in a brothel owned by Pamelia Mann, whose story is told next. In 1857 Dickinson married William Hannig and moved to Austin, where they lived together, apparently happily, until her death in 1883. ★

Pamelia Mann

Pamelia Mann's small part in Texas history is an oddly funny story in the midst of war. On the march east, Houston stopped at Groce's Plantation to train his troops. While there, he confiscated Mann's two oxen to pull the cannon he had somehow obtained. Houston assured the good woman he planned to turn east, toward Nacogdoches and safety. When Mann found he had instead turned the troops toward Harrisburg and the Mexican army, she caught up with Houston and, using her horse to block his so he couldn't ignore her, demanded her oxen. He refused, and she suddenly pulled out a knife, slashed the leather straps binding the animals to the cannon, and, brandishing a whip, drove them away. Houston stared in amazement.

When the wagon master told Houston he couldn't pull the cannon without them and was going after her, Houston supposedly said, "Well, good luck. You'll need it. That woman will fight."

Legend has it that the wagon master returned, late at night, limping, his shirt in shreds, refusing to talk about what had happened. But he didn't have the oxen.

After her brief moment of fame, Mann's story is similar to Susanna Dickinson's in that it's not pretty. She established the Mansion House Hotel in Houston, which was the "site of much boomtown rowdiness," according to *The Handbook of Texas Online*. Other sources outright call it a brothel. She was indicted for crimes ranging from larceny and assault to fornication and convicted of forgery—a conviction that carried an automatic death penalty at the time. President Mirabeau B. Lamar granted her executive clemency.

Apparently, for all her peccadilloes, Mrs. Mann had friends in high places. When her son married in a ceremony held at the Mansion House, Sam Houston was the best man, assisted by Ashbel Smith, a pioneering doctor who was surgeon general to the Army of the Republic.

Mann died in Houston in 1840 of yellow fever, leaving an estate of more than $40,000—quite large for the place and time. ★

Emily Morgan
the "Yellow Rose of Texas"

The story of Emily Morgan, heroine of the Battle of San Jacinto, is a wonderful example of the way Texans shape myths and legends to suit what they want to believe.

Sam Houston's Army of the Republic camped on the plains at San Jacinto, directly across from Santa Anna's Federales. In spite of the urgency his troops felt, Houston did not attack. He sat in his tent, read maps, took messages, called for Erastus "Deaf" Smith—but didn't attack. This went on for several days, and the troops were ready each morning for a pre-dawn attack. Instead, when he attacked,

Houston charged the Mexicans in mid-afternoon, when they were taking their traditional siesta.

That's where Emily Morgan comes in. She was supposedly a mulatto slave, in Santa Anna's tent with him, keeping his thoughts away from battle. In fact, some stories say he couldn't struggle into his pants fast enough to respond to the attack. Other versions make it sound like Emily was only doing her patriotic duty.

The truth? Her name was Emily West, not Morgan, and she was a free African-American woman who had come from Connecticut under contract to work for a year as a housekeeper for James Morgan, proprietor of a hotel in New Washington, Texas. On April 16, she and several other servants were kidnapped by Mexican soldiers, along with residents and workmen. Santa Anna arrived in New Washington, stayed three days, burned the town, and headed for San Jacinto. Morgan, probably by then a rape victim, was forced to accompany the Mexican troops.

She may well have been in Santa Anna's tent, but she could not have known Houston's plans. After the battle, she was taken in by a Texian soldier. She remained in Texas until 1837, when she returned to her home in Connecticut.

The story of her part in defeating the Mexican army was promoted by a visiting Englishman, William Bollaert, who recorded it in his journal and no doubt spread it abroad. Morgan's story was picked up by journalists, who gave it further credence. The story seemed to grow and is today part of Texas' folklore, though many will tell you it's part of Texas history.

Texans have kept the legend alive. In the 1950s bandleader Mitch Miller popularized the song, "The Yellow Rose of Texas," and folklorist and journalist Francis X. Tolbert suggested that Emily Morgan was a fitting candidate for the identity of the girl in the song, presumably because Morgan was a mulatto. There is an Emily Morgan Hotel in San Antonio, but there is no existing picture of Emily Morgan. ★

AN INDIAN CAPTIVE

Children across the western frontier were kidnapped by the Plains Indians. Relatively few lived their lives as "white Indians"; some were killed; many returned home after varying periods of time. Often those who were returned to their families had a difficult time adapting to white culture after having lived with the Indians. ★

CYNTHIA ANN PARKER

BUT TEXAS, WHICH SAW dozens of children taken, can boast the most famous captive: Cynthia Ann Parker.

Parker was born in Illinois about 1825 and was nine or ten when her family moved to Central Texas. They settled on the Navasota River in Limestone County, between the present cities of Groesbeck and Mexia. On May 19, 1836, a raiding party of Comanche, Kiowa, and Kichai, attacked the fort, killing Parker's father and other men at the fort. They took her, her brother, and three others. All but Parker were released soon after.

Some stories say that she was staked on the prairie at night to test her courage. Whatever the truth, she apparently pleased the Comanche enough that they decided to adopt her. She was given to a childless couple and was raised as a Comanche girl.

Several attempts were made to secure her freedom. In the 1840s, her brother begged her to return to her family, but she told him she loved her Comanche parents too much to leave them. Later, when asked to return, she would say no, she loved her husband, Chief Peta Nocona, and her sons too much to leave. The Comanche refused to release her. Married to a chief, she was considered an important part of the tribe.

Parker was with the Comanche twenty-five years until 1860, when Lawrence Sullivan Ross of the Texas Rangers

Cynthia Ann Parker.
Courtesy Fort Worth Museum of Science and History.

15

attacked a hunting camp on a tributary of the Pease River in North Central Texas. The Rangers captured three Indians and noticed that one, a woman clutching an infant, had blue eyes. Supposedly she said in broken English, "Me Cynthia Ann." The infant was her daughter, Topsannah (often called Prairie Flower in English). Parker was afraid her husband and sons—Quanah and Pecos—were dead. She would later learn that Peta Nocona, the warrior chief who was her husband, was indeed dead, but her sons lived.

Isaac Parker identified her as his niece and took her and Topsannah to his home in the Birdville community, northeast of Fort Worth. She went on the condition that her sons would be sent to her if they were found. As the small party passed through Fort Worth, a now-famous photo of Parker was taken. She had chopped off her hair, the Comanche sign of mourning, and is clutching her daughter. She looks absolutely miserable.

Parker never adjusted to the Anglo way of life and remained an embarrassment to her family. All she wanted was to go home to her Comanche family.

Prairie Flower or Topsannah died and is buried in a cemetery in Van Zandt County. In the early 1870s, Parker died, many say of a broken heart. She was buried in East Texas but her son Quanah had her body moved to the small cemetery in Cache in the Indian Territory. Later her body was moved again, and she was buried next to Quanah.

Quanah Parker's life exemplified his dual Indian/

Anglo heritage. He was instrumental in leading the last Comanche onto the reservation and helping them adjust to their new way of life. By bringing together Comanche and whites, he honored both his parents. ★

RANCH WOMEN

A lot of Texas women have lived on ranches, and some of their stories have become legendary. There are, for instance, the women of the JA Ranch in Palo Duro Canyon. ★

MOLLY GOODNIGHT AND CORNELIA ADAIR

MOLLY GOODNIGHT AND her husband, Charles—who became probably the most famous rancher in Texas— were ranching in Pueblo, Colorado, when John Adair backed Charles financially to establish the JA Ranch in Palo Duro Canyon in the Panhandle. The two couples drove cattle from Pueblo to the ranch, Molly Goodnight driving a wagon and Cornelia Adair riding horseback.

The Adairs were absentee partners, while Charles Goodnight managed the ranch. His wife helped with the ranch chores as well as running their household. The

Molly Goodnight. *Courtesy Panhandle Plains Historical Museum, Canyon, Texas.*

nearest female neighbor was miles away, and they saw each other maybe once every six to twelve months. But her friends were the cowboys and a few curious Indians. She kept chickens as pets and rescued baby buffalo whose mothers had been killed by buffalo hunters. In fact, her efforts established the Goodnight buffalo herd which became important to preserving the breed from extinction. And the ranch also experimented with crossbreeding cattle and buffalo, resulting in a "cattalo."

Molly Goodnight became known as both the First Lady of Palo Duro (she was the only woman on the ranch) and the Mother of the Panhandle, because she was doctor, nurse, homemaker, sister, mother, and confidante to the ranch hands, who adored her. When Charles was

Cornelia Adair. *Courtesy Panhandle Plains Historical Museum, Canyon, Texas.*

away, she managed the ranch's affairs, but mostly, like so many other women, she was a ranch wife while her husband managed the land and cattle.

Cornelia Adair was cut of different cloth. Born an American, she was a naturalized British citizen and widowed when she met John Adair, also a British citizen. But from the time her husband went into partnership with Charles Goodnight in 1877, she became actively involved in the JA Ranch. When he died in 1885, she became Charles' partner, and in 1887 she bought out his interest, including land, livestock, equipment, and rights to the JA brand. She ran the ranch and managed its business affairs, and by 1917, it encompassed a half million acres.

19

Cornelia Adair spent most of her time in Ireland, where she and her late husband had a baronial home, but she kept a home in Clarendon, Texas, not far from the ranch, by Texas distances. And she visited the ranch annually, always riding out with the cowboys. She may have been an absentee landlord but when she was there, she was a hands-on ranch manager. ★

Henrietta King. Portrait of a Texas Lady *by Patrick Messersmith.* *Found in* Henrietta King: Rancher and Philanthropist *by Judy Alter (State House Press, 2005).*

HENRIETTA KING

HENRIETTA KING WAS NOT a native Texan, and her life living on and eventually managing one of the largest ranches in the country seems almost an accident. She was born in Missouri in 1832. When her mother died, her minister-father sent her to a boarding school and she was expected to follow the family pattern and marry a minister.

King's father moved his family to Brownsville, Texas, in 1849. Family lore says they lived on a houseboat docked in the space boat captain Richard King thought reserved for his ship. Her first meeting with King was not pleasant according to family lore—when King saw another boat where he usually docked his, he began swearing at the boat. Henrietta came on deck of the houseboat and scolded him for indecent language. The legend is that he fell in love with her at that moment.

She was engaged to another man—some say a banker—but she broke off the engagement after Richard King proposed. King saw his future bride as often as he could. He was protective of her, making sure not to walk her on the street in front of rowdy bars and uncivilized citizens of the border town. He even started attending the church where her father preached.

But he was often away, delivering supplies along the Rio Grande or exploring the South Texas brush country where he bought land. Once, King bought most of the livestock available in the Mexican town of Cruillas, leaving many of the townspeople no way of earning a living. Most of the townspeople moved with him to Texas in one big procession remembered as *la entrada*. These people became known as *Los Kineños*, the "King men," and some of their descendants still live on King Ranch.

Richard and Henrietta married December 10, 1854, and went to his Santa Gertrudis Ranch for their honeymoon. The ranch had a few *jacales* (thatched-roof

21

huts made of sticks and mud daub), mesquite corrals, a commissary with a lean-to attached, which may have been where Henrietta lived. There was a separate kitchen, a blockhouse, a dormitory for visitors, and a watchtower. Farther out were stables and sheds, a blacksmith's shop, and houses where employees lived. *Los Kineños* called her *La Patrona* because she took care of them and their children, although she was strict with them. She allowed no cursing or drinking..

Richard King was a loyal southerner. During the Civil War, when Union ships blockaded Brownsville, he carried cotton across the ranch in wagons to Mexico and British ships in the Gulf of Mexico. He also rounded up cattle to ship to England. When Union soldiers attacked the ranch looking for him, he was in Mexico rounding up stolen cattle. The oft-told story is that the soldiers killed Mrs. King's bodyguard, destroyed the house, and stole livestock. The Union forces then put Henrietta and her family in a carriage, and she went to a friend's home in San Patricio where she gave birth to Robert Lee King. She and the children, along with her father, went to San Antonio as soon as she was able. They spent the rest of the war there, uncertain where Captain King was. (He was actually serving as a private in the Confederate Army.) When they were reunited, King gave her a pair of diamond earrings. She wore them the rest of her life, although after his death she had them capped as a sign of mourning.

The ranch prospered in the years of cattle drives,

but when the Kings lost their son, Robert Lee King, to pneumonia in 1883, Captain King decided to sell the land. Henrietta is said to have reminded him of his lesson to her: "Never sell." In 1885, Captain King died of stomach cancer, leaving everything to his wife—most people believe it was about half a million acres of land and $1.5 million in debt. She hired Robert Kleberg, a lawyer who had worked with Captain King and who later married her daughter Alice, to run the King Ranch. Kleberg began to pay off the debt and buy more land. An innovative rancher, he and his sons developed Santa Gertrudis cattle, a cross of Brahman and Shorthorn that thrived in South Texas, dipped cattle into vats to prevent ticks, and proved that artesian wells could bring water to dry South Texas By then her grandsons, Richard and Robert, Jr. and her son, Robert, Sr., were active in the ranch management.

To get cattle to market, Henrietta King and several other ranchers supplied the capital that built the St. Louis, Brownsville & Mexico Railway. The train, which cut across her property, first ran July 4, 1904. She donated land in the middle of her ranch to the Kleberg Town & Improvement Company for the town of Kingsville but allowed no saloons nor liquor. Indeed, liquor could not be brought in to Kleberg County until the 1990s. By 1905, Kingsville had a population of almost one thousand. Henrietta King owned the Kingsville Lumber Company, the weekly newspaper, and the Gulf Coast Cotton

Gin Company. She built an icehouse, so farmers could preserve their produce, donated the land and funds for the construction of a Presbyterian Church, and donated the land to any congregation that wished to build a place of worship. A first public school opened, but it was soon too small for the number of students. King donated land for the high school.

In 1912, the Big House at the Santa Gertrudis Division burned. King built a new, larger, fireproof house. During the 1916 uprisings in Mexico, *bandidos* stole livestock and killed King Ranch cowboys. The ranch was raided twenty-six times, but she refused to leave.

Henrietta King died in 1925. At her ranch funeral, the procession started at the main residence, where her body had lain in state, traveled to the Chamberlain Cemetery in Kingsville, for which she had donated the land. All the *Kineños* attended, cantering around the open grave once, hats at their sides in a final salute.

Henrietta King left her family—and Texas—a remarkable legacy because of her philanthropy in the establishment of towns, schools, churches, and hospitals. Today, King Ranch is a family-owned corporation, run by a board of directors with a majority of non-family members. Descendants of Henrietta and Richard King gather at the ranch for a reunion annually. ★

Electra Waggoner. *Courtesy Historic Fort Worth, Inc.*

Electra Waggoner

THE WAGGONER FAMILY of the Three D is one of the most famous ranching families in Texas and certainly the one with the most colorful women. Electra Waggoner Wharton, whose beautiful home and lavish lifestyle were the talk of Fort Worth in the first decade of the twentieth century, was the most public, but they were a family of women who illustrate just how tough ranch women could be—cowboys aren't the only ones who make the myths and legends.

Electra grew up on the Waggoner ranch, riding as hard as any cowboy. After time at a finishing school, she fell in love with Max Lingo, who was in the lumber business in Dallas. Apparently her parents did not approve of Mr. Lingo, for when he asked Electra to marry him, they convinced her to take a world tour. In Europe, she met and fell in love with A. B. Wharton, Jr., a Philadelphia socialite. The year she returned from her tour, 1901, the town of Electra in North Central Texas was named in her honor. The town had alternately been called Beaver and Waggoner. Tom Waggoner did not want the town named Waggoner, and citizens were unhappy with Beaver. So they voted to call their small town, which would later have multiple oil derricks, Electra.

Electra and A. B. were married at her family's home, El Castile in Decatur, in June 1902. Their honeymoon was an extended tour of Europe, after which they planned to settle in Philadelphia. The story varies on whether the newlyweds bought property themselves at 1509 Pennsylvania in Fort Worth or W. T. Waggoner bought it and built them a "honeymoon cottage" to persuade them not to leave Fort Worth. In 1904 they moved into the house with their infant son. Electra called the house "Rubusmont," which means Thistle Hill, because it sat on a hill, nicely situated to catch the Texas breezes.

The years in Thistle Hill established Electra's international reputation for lavish living and glamour. Legend says that she was the first to spend $20,000 in a one-day shopping spree at Neiman-Marcus; the next day she returned to spend almost as much for things she had overlooked the previous day. She had fresh flowers delivered to her house daily, and ordered the latest clothes from New York and Paris—though she often returned those that didn't please her. Supposedly, she refused to try on a dress that anyone else had tried on—and she never wore the same outfit twice. The closets at Thistle Hill bulged with furs and fine gowns. At one time, she was said to own 350 pairs of shoes.

The Whartons entertained frequently, and the newspapers of the day reported every detail. In 1906, there was a "phantom dance" for Halloween; guests wore pillowcases and sheets, and the only lighting came from candles in pumpkins. The same year there was an old-fashioned candy pull and an "al fresco" party on the verandah, with card games, professional vaudeville performers, and lunch for two hundred people. One New Year's the couple invited 160 friends to a party held in the third-floor ballroom, which was decorated with smilax and tinsel.

The Whartons sold Thistle Hill to Winton Scott in 1911 and built a new home, Zacaweista ("long grasses" in Comanche) on the property she had recently inherited from her father. They divorced in 1919, and Electra moved to Dallas, marrying twice more before her untimely death in 1925 at the age of forty-three. ★

Tad Lucas with her daughter, Mitzi. *Courtesy National Cowgirl Museum and Hall of Fame, Fort Worth, Texas.*

Tad Lucas, Cowgirl

NOT ALL TEXAS WOMEN involved with cattle stayed on the ranch—some went on to become competitive performers on the Wild West show and rodeo circuit. Tad Lucas of Fort Worth was probably the best trick rider the rodeo ever produced. She was born in 1902 on a ranch outside Cody, Nebraska, and nicknamed Tad because she was the youngest of twenty-four children. Growing up, she always had brothers and sisters to play with—and their games usually involved horses. Like most ranch children, she rode bareback, which helped her develop a sense of balance and timing. She was put to work at an early age—roping, helping with branding, rounding up cattle, and all the chores that go with ranching.

Lucas came to rodeo the way the event started—by riding wild cows and outlaw stock brought to town by ranchers on Saturdays. She competed against other ranch children and local Sioux Indian children. Ranchers would ear down the stock—hold them by the ears—until the rider was mounted and then let go. If a rider's performance was good, the hat was passed and proceeds raised, though the money was usually given to the Red Cross. When she was fifteen or sixteen, she exercised horses for a neighbor, and he took her to the fair in Cody as his jockey. She saw that there was a $25 prize for girls in the steer riding competition and entered it, though she'd never ridden a steer before. She won.

In the early 1920s she joined Colonel Frank Hatley's Wild West show, where she learned to trick ride. In 1923, with that show, she rode a Brahma (she pronounced it Bray-mer) steer in Madison Square Garden, the only woman to ride a Brahma in that setting. She also tried riding saddle broncs. She was good at it, because she'd been riding rough stock all her life.

In 1924 she was part of a troupe that went to England for an exhibition. A month before they sailed, she married bronc rider Buck Lucas. The England trip was their honeymoon. When the newlyweds returned from England, they bought a home on Roberts Cutoff Road in the northwest part of Fort Worth. It would be their home the rest of their lives.

Tad Lucas' star was on the rise. She won the trick riding championship in 1925 and for the next six years. That same year, she was the All Around Champion in

Chicago. At New York's Madison Square Garden, she was All Around Champion and Trick Riding Champion for eight years, setting a new record. Because she won three years in a row—1928–1930—she was given permanent possession of the Metro-Goldwyn-Mayer Trophy, worth some $10,000. Lucas even won honors in Australia. From the mid-1920s through the early 1940s, she and her husband owned and operated the Triangle Rodeo Company. But during World War II, women's contests disappeared from the rodeo circuit.

Lucas' daughter, Mitzi (now Mitzi Lucas Riley) was born in 1930, when Lucas was at the height of her fame. Mitzi rode in the grand entry parades when she was still an infant; at two, she was given her own pony; at five, she was doing some tricks. Rodeo was in the family blood. Mitzi Riley went on to earn fame as a cowgirl in her own right.

Tad Lucas had her share of wrecks. The worst was in Chicago at the World's Fair. Lucas was known for doing tricks that other cowgirls wouldn't dare attempt, and one of them was going under the horse's belly. But in 1933 in Chicago, she slipped and was caught in the horse's hooves, unable to free herself for several seconds. She broke her arm so severely that doctors told her she would lose it. She refused amputation, saying she'd rather die; then they told her she would never ride again. Within a year, she proved them wrong, riding with her left arm in a heavy cast, which limited the tricks she could do. She had that cast for three years and had seven operations. The rest of her life she had limited motion in her left hand and arm, which was shorter than her right.

Tad Lucas never competed in trick riding after she broke her arm. She could do many exhibition tricks with one arm, but she wasn't ready for competition. She acted as a rodeo official and sometimes even as a clown, but she didn't compete. She retired from rodeo in 1958, when her trick-riding horse was getting old, and she didn't want to break in another.

Tad Lucas was honored by the National Rodeo Hall of Fame, the National Cowgirl Hall of Fame, and the ProRodeo Hall of Fame. She lived in the Fort Worth home she and her husband built until her death in 1990. Established in her will, the Tad Lucas Memorial Award honors women who excel in any field related to western heritage. ★

THE ALAMO AGAIN

By the 1890s the Alamo was a shambles, almost beyond repair. Souvenir hunters chipped away pieces of the sculptures, stole whole figures and left others headless, and carved pieces from the cedar paneled doors. The historic site was saved by two women with very different ideas about the mission and its use. They were Adina de Zavala and Clara Driscoll. ★

Adina de Zavala. *Courtesy Texas State Library and Archives Commission*

ADINA DE ZAVALA

ADINA DE ZAVALA BROUGHT a tradition of Texas history to her lifetime career as a protector of Texas treasures and leader in establishing statewide recognition of Texas' Independence Day on March 2. The granddaughter of Lorenzo de Zavala, a Mexican citizen who became the first vice president of the provisional government of the Republic of Texas, she was born in 1861 within sight of the battlefield at San Jacinto. Later the family moved to the San Antonio area. De Zavala was educated at Sam Houston Normal Institute (now Sam Houston State University) and then at a music school in Missouri. She taught in Terrell, Texas, and then in the later 1880s in San Antonio, where she began her preservation efforts.

De Zavala organized a group of women to "keep green the memory of heroes, founders, and pioneers of Texas." The group became the de Zavala Chapter of the Daughters of the Republic of Texas and focused on four missions south of the city as well as on the Alamo.

She enlisted the help of Pompeo Coppini, the Italian-born sculptor who created the monuments that front the Alamo. She asked merchants to donate bricks, lumber, cedar posts, and wire to repair the mission. De Zavala considered the *convento* or long barracks particularly important because the bloodiest fighting of the Battle of the Alamo took place there, not in the chapel as many wrongly believed. The long barracks were privately owned, and she tried to get them under state control. (The State of Texas already owned the mission church.)

Just as the barracks were about to go on sale, the de Zavala chapter of the DRT welcomed a new member: Clara Driscoll, daughter of a wealthy rancher, oilman, banker, and developer. Driscoll provided $500 to secure an option to purchase the property and eventually paid $65,000 to save it (she was later repaid by the state). Private contributions to the cause were less than $10,000.

The two women disagreed about use of the site, with Driscoll wanting to remove the remaining *convento* walls and de Zavala so desperate to preserve them that in 1908 she barricaded herself in the building to protest probable destruction of the structure. The sheriff visited but could neither force her out nor enforce his ban on allowing

33

anyone to bring her food and water. de Zavala's reasoning was that she had heard that "possession is nine points in the law." Newspapers throughout the country featured the story, and de Zavala was banished from the DRT in which Driscoll held much power. In 1913, the upper story of the long barracks was destroyed but the remaining structure is a part of the Alamo complex today.

In 1912 de Zavala organized the Texas Historical and Landmarks Association, which placed thirty-eight markers at historic sites. She helped save the Spanish Governors' Palace in San Antonio, and she located the sites of the first two missions established in Texas by the Spanish.

De Zavala also had a career as a writer, developing a short play about Texas' six flags to help her students learn about their Texas heritage. Her idea of "Texas Under Six Flags" caused the San Antonio Conservation Society to restore homes representative of the six governments whose flags had flown over Texas: Spain, France, Mexico, the Republic of Texas, the United States, and the Confederate States of America. She also wrote numerous newspaper articles and the book, *History and Legends of the Alamo and Other Missions*. A charter member of the Texas State Historical Association, she donated her large collection of documents to the Center for American History at the University of Texas in Austin.

In 1955, two months after her death, the Texas Legislature honored her, and in 1994 the DRT dedicated a special Commemorative Marker at her gravesite. Also in 1994, the Bexar County Historical Commission was granted approval to put a State Historical Marker in Alamo Plaza to honor "The First Lady of Texas Historic Preservation." ★

Clara Driscoll. *Courtesy The Daughters of the Republic of Texas Library, Gift of Mrs. L. T. Barrow. CN96.002.*

CLARA DRISCOLL

CLARA DRISCOLL IS KNOWN AS the "Savior of the Alamo" because she had the financial resources that Adina de Zavala lacked, and she wasn't afraid to use them to save the Alamo.

Born near Corpus Christi, she was the daughter of a rancher, oilman, and developer. Like de Zavala, she was part of a family with a long Texas history—both her grandfathers had fought in the Texas Revolution. Driscoll was sent abroad to study and travel, but she returned to Texas at the age of eighteen and soon developed an interest in preserving historic sites in Texas. She worked with the Daughters of the Republic of Texas to preserve the Alamo—which means she paid almost the entire price to purchase the long barracks from the commercial grocery firm that was about to sell it to a hotel developer. In 1905, the state of Texas repaid her investment in the Alamo, took ownership of the property, and conveyed it to the DRT. Unlike de Zavala, Driscoll thought the long barracks should be demolished. She envisioned a park-like setting with a focus on the church. The DRT split into two factions, one led by de Zavala and the other by Driscoll. In several legal decisions, state courts supported Driscoll's point of view—she and her group mistakenly thought that the long barracks had been constructed after the 1836 battle. In the resulting disagreement, the DRT dissolved its ties with de Zavala.

But Clara Driscoll did not devote all her energy to the DRT and the Alamo. She had other interests. She wrote a novel, *The Girl of La Gloria*, a collection of short stories, *In the Shadow of the Alamo*, and a comic opera. In 1906 she married New Yorker Henry Hulme Sevier and made her home in New York City. But when her father died, the couple returned to Texas so that she could help manage her father's financial interests. Her husband founded the *Austin American-Statesman*, still Austin's major daily newspaper, and she became active in several public affairs groups, including the Daughters of the Republic of Texas, where she served as president. She was responsible for the construction of Laguna Gloria, an Italianate mansion that later became the original home of the Austin Museum of Art.

When Driscoll's brother died in 1929, she and her husband moved to the family ranch in South Texas so that they could manage the family land and petroleum holdings. She was able to double the value of the estate. In 1935, she and her husband were divorced, and she was known forever afterwards as Mrs. Clara Driscoll.

Driscoll was involved in a variety of civic activities—liquidating the mortgage on the clubhouse of the Texas Federation of Women's Clubs, serving on the Texas Centennial Exposition executive board, and constructing a hotel, the Hotel Robert Driscoll, in Corpus Christi, to memorialize her brother and improve the economic life of that city.

Clara Driscoll, an outspoken Democrat, was also active politically. She served as the party's national committeewoman from Texas for sixteen years, beginning in 1922. In 1939, she supported John Nance Garner for president, and in 1944 she backed President Franklin D. Roosevelt's unprecedented bid for a fourth term.

Clara Driscoll died in 1945 in Corpus Christi. Her body lay in state in the Alamo chapel, and she was buried in the Masonic Cemetery in San Antonio. She never reconciled with Adina de Zavala. ★

AUTHORS

Texas has a tradition of women writers that stretches back over 150 years to the first visitors to the state and includes countless names, some well known, others most obscure. Two or three deserve special mention here. ★

KATHERINE ANNE PORTER

IF KATHERINE ANNE PORTER was Texas' greatest woman author, she was also one of the country's greatest authors, ranking with William Faulkner, Ernest Hemingway, Eudora Welty, and others. She was a Texan who left Texas and became more embittered about her home state as the years went on. But in the end, she returned.

She was born Callie Russell Porter in Indian Creek, in 1890, though she sometimes gave the date as 1894. She grew up in Kyle, near Austin. Her mother had died when she was two; her father seemed never to hold a job, but he took his children to his mother, the strong and determined Catharine Ann Porter. Young Callie grew up listening to her grandmother's stories of the

Katherine Anne Porter. *Courtesy Papers of Katherine Anne Porter, Special Collections, University of Maryland Libraries.*

Civil War and her family's past. The family was poor, and rumors say that the girl and her sisters and one brother often wore neighbors' cast-off clothes. In later life, she sometimes misrepresented her childhood, portraying herself as the southern-belle daughter of a cultured and affluent family.

Her grandmother died when Porter was eleven, and the young girl spent a year in a school in San Antonio. Beyond that she had little formal education except elementary school. At sixteen, she ran away from a convent in New Orleans to marry the first of four husbands. She was married to John Koontz for nine years, living with him only seven and accusing him of abuse in the divorce filing. The most important thing to come out of her marriage was her conversion to Catholicism, which she practiced off and on thereafter. She asked, at the divorce, that her name be legally changed to Katherine Anne Porter, no doubt a tribute to her grandmother.

Thereafter she was diagnosed with tuberculosis and eventually spent two years in a sanitarium where she met and was befriended by Kitty Barry Crawford and her husband, J. Garfield Crawford, from Fort Worth. With their help, she spent brief periods in Fort Worth, both writing and acting. But Porter did not settle down easily. She began writing in Fort Wayne, Indiana, for a publication called *The Critic*; then she moved to Denver, where she almost died during the 1918 influenza epidemic. Then it was on to Greenwich Village, where she did ghostwriting and wrote children's stories and publicity for a motion picture company. Porter shifted to Mexico in 1920, but by 1921 she was back in New York.

In 1922 Porter published her first short story, "Maria Conception," in *Century* magazine. It reflected her experiences in Mexico and was also the beginning of a publishing career that while slim in its entirety was significant in its quality. Her stories appeared mostly in small magazines, and her first collection of stories, *Flowering Judas*, was limited to only 600 copies. Critics took more notice of her next book, *Pale Horse, Pale Rider* (1939), consisting of three novellas, the title story reflecting her experience with influenza. She published two collections of essays in the 1950s, and her *Collected Short Stories* (1965) earned her a Pulitzer.

Porter's lone novel is *Ship of Fools*, which appeared when she was seventy-two, though she'd been working on it for fifteen years, as the literary world waited in anticipation. Some say her career rests on that dark novel; others claim it is not her best work. The novel is set on a mixed freighter/passenger ship, with passengers from many countries, each representing evil in this life as she found it in people.

In 1977, she published *The Never-Ending Wrong*, an account of the Sacco-Vanzetti trial, some fifty years after she had protested that trial. By then her health was failing, and she published no more. She died in New York in 1980.

Porter's bitterness about Texas began in 1939 when the Texas Institute of Letters gave its first annual prize to J. Frank Dobie's *Apache Gold and Yaqui Silver*, instead of *Pale Horse, Pale Rider*. Her bitterness deepened when she was a lecturer at the University of Texas-Austin and understood that Chancellor Harry Ransom meant to name the Humanities Research Center or some part of it for her and set up a Katherine Anne Porter Room. No one knows whether she misunderstood or Ransom unknowingly encouraged her belief, but she was devastated when it did not happen. (Today the center is the Harry Ransom Center.) She did, however, accept an honorary degree from Howard Payne University in Brownwood in 1976.

And ultimately she came home. Her ashes are buried next to her mother in the Indian Creek cemetery. ★

Dorothy Scarborough.
Courtesy The Texas Collection, Baylor University.

DOROTHY SCARBOROUGH

DOROTHY SCARBOROUGH actually predates Katherine Anne Porter, but while Porter's reputation was national in scope, Scarborough remained a regional writer and is best known for one novel—*The Wind*. That novel eclipses her many and varied other accomplishments.

Dorothy Scarborough was an important Texas folklorist, an early and lifetime member of the Texas Folklore Society, of which she served as president in 1914–1915. Her interests were in folksongs, cowboys, and Negro folklore, and she published two major folklore collections, *On the Trail of Negro Folksongs* and *A Song Catcher in the Southern Mountains* (posthumous). She also wrote nonfiction—*From a Southern Porch*—and a scholarly study, *The Supernatural in Modern Fiction*, her dissertation, which launched her on a career of writing about ghosts.

But her main interest was fiction. Scarborough never denied her Texas roots. Indeed she felt a strong tie to the land and people of Texas. Three of her novels—*In the Land of Cotton, Can't Get a Redbird,* and *The Stretch-Berry Smile*, deal with the hard life of cotton sharecroppers in and around Waco and reveal her thorough knowledge of that way of life. In 1933, she wrote a children's book, *The Story of Cotton*, which covers every step of cotton production.

Her landmark novel, *The Wind*, is set in Sweetwater during the drought of the mid-1880s and dramatizes the toll that wind and drought can take on a fragile woman. The heroine, Letty, is eventually driven to murder and suicide. The novel was published anonymously, and Texans were outraged, believing that a northerner had written this negative book about conditions in Texas, at a time when Texans prided themselves on the mystique of their state. When Scarborough was revealed as the author, attitudes softened a bit, but the novel is still controversial in the state. In spite of the controversy, it is considered a Texas classic and earned Scarborough a place as one of Texas' leading women authors.

Unlike Porter, Scarborough did not return to Texas. She died, unexpectedly, in her sleep, in New York, of a heart attack in 1935. She was working on *A Songcatcher in the Southern Mountains* at the time. Outside Texas, her reputation, if it survives, is as an authority on folksong in the United States. In Texas, she's the woman who wrote *The Wind.* ★

JANE GILMORE RUSHING

NOVELIST AND SHORT STORY WRITER Jane Gilmore Rushing focused on life in West Texas. It was the life she knew from childhood. Born in Pyron, between Snyder and Sweetwater, she earned a BA in 1944, an MA in 1945, and a PhD in 1957 from Texas Tech University. She was a newspaper reporter, high school teacher, and college professor, and lived most of her life in Lubbock.

Rushing's novels are *Mary Dove: A Love Story*, set in the mid-nineteenth century and telling the story of the love of a young interracial couple; *Tamzen*, based on a conflict over land ownership that pits small farmers against ranchers; *Walnut Grove*, about a developing community trying to attract a railroad; *Winds of Blame,* about a community that covers up a crime; *Against the Moon*, which brings several generations of women to the bedside of a dying grandmother, who helps the women see their own lives clearly without regard to the self-righteousness of their community (Rushing was no cheerleader for the moral atmosphere in small towns); and *The Raincrow,* a contemporary novel set in a West Texas town that is dying. Once again the oldest character is the wisest and leads the younger ones.

Rushing wrote one novel set in New England, *Covenant of Grace*, a fictionalized account of Anne Hutchinson, but she remains a Texas novelist who was able to move beyond the particulars of her region to deal with universal themes. Her reputation is not as secure as Porter's nor does she have the one outstanding novel to mark her career, but she deserves to be among the top in the list of Texas women authors. ★

IN THE PUBLIC EYE

BESSIE COLEMAN, A PILOT

TEXAS HAS HAD its share of women who lived on the edge, from trail drivers to outlaws and rodeo riders. But one of the most unusual was Bessie Coleman, who was the first black woman in the world licensed to fly as a pilot. Of course, she had to leave not only Texas but the United States to learn to fly.

Coleman first remembered seeing planes when she was a young girl picking cotton near Waxahachie. She looked up at planes flying overhead and vowed that someday she

too would fly one. She was ten years old when the Wright brothers flew at Kitty Hawk, and reading about them inspired her more. She finished school, did one semester of college, and went to Chicago to live with a brother, always scheming to save money to learn to fly. School after school rejected her—she was black and female. Finally, with the help of a patron, she went to France to learn to fly.

In 1921 she was licensed. Within a year she was learning to do stunts and aerobatic flying. When she came back to New York in 1922, a headline read "Negro Aviatrix Arrives." Air shows were popular in the United States in those days, and Coleman drew large crowds when she did figure-eights, loop-the-loop, and the Richtofen glide, where she cut the engine, let the plane glide, and then pulled it up into barrel rolls. People came because they were curious about a black woman flying a plane.

Coleman dreamed of opening a flight school for African Americans, because she remembered how frustrated she had been. When she did a show in her hometown of Waxahachie, she insisted that there not be separate entrances for whites and blacks. But when she flew over the field, she saw that the audience had been divided by color.

She had close calls. Once her engine lost power, and the plane began diving toward the earth. Even she thought she would crash, but she kept cranking it, and the engine caught. Another time she was lost when the lights on her plane failed. She landed in a field. In a 1925 crash, she broke ribs and a leg and had cuts and bruises, but a year later she was back in the air.

In 1926 Coleman was flying at a show in Florida when her plane flipped over. She fell out to her death. An investigation showed that a wrench had been jammed between the plane's gears and may have caused the plane to flip. No one understands why Coleman, a careful pilot, was not strapped into her seat.

Bessie Coleman was twenty-nine years old when she died, but she had spent her adult life doing what she loved, living on the edge. On the anniversary of her death, black pilots fly over her Chicago grave and drop flowers. In 1995, the government issued a postal stamp with her picture on it, giving her a much-deserved place in history. ★

Mary Martin. *Doss Heritage and Cultural Center,
Weatherford, Texas.*

Mary Martin, Entertainer

Texas was home for the actress credited with bringing significance to the roles of performers in musical comedy. But her career did not begin on such an auspicious note.

When showman Billy Rose was auditioning candidates for his Casa Mañana production in Fort Worth in 1936, he turned away a young singer and dancer from Weatherford, Texas. Rose told her she was too good for the chorus but not good enough for feature billing. Then he said, "I'm not running an amateur show—come back when you've made a name for yourself." The young girl was Mary Martin, and within two years she was singing "My Heart Belongs to Daddy" in Cole Porter's *Leave It to Me* on Broadway.

Mary Martin was born in Weatherford in 1913, the daughter of an attorney and a violin teacher. Performing seemed to be in her blood early on, and she began voice lessons at twelve. Her first marriage, entered into when she was seventeen, ended in divorce. Her son, Larry Hagman, was born in 1931; Hagman went on to be an actor, best known for his TV roles in "I Dream of Jeannie" and "Dallas."

Martin began her professional career singing on radio in Dallas and dancing at Los Angeles nightclubs, but she could not break into the film industry. *Leave It to Me* was her big break, and Broadway audiences loved her. After that, Hollywood came calling, and she appeared in several major films for Paramount Pictures. She also appeared on NBC and CBS in such shows as "Kraft Music Hall."

Martin married again, to Richard Halliday, who became her manager, and they had a daughter. She returned to Broadway where she appeared in several shows, the most notable of which were the 1947 production of *Annie, Get Your Gun* and the 1949 production of *South Pacific*, in which she starred opposite Ezio Pinza. After two years in London with *South Pacific*, she was back on Broadway and television. Her roles included her famous characterization of Peter Pan, which some critics called her best performance ever. She herself said the role was her favorite.

Martin won Tony Awards for her work in *Peter Pan* and *The Sound of Music*, toured with *Hello, Dolly!* for military audiences in Asia, appeared on Broadway again in *I Do, I Do*, but her career was winding down. She and her husband spent much of their time at their ranch in Brazil. After his death in the late 1940s, she made a comeback on Broadway and in touring productions, sometimes playing an aging actress.

Mary Martin won an award from the John F. Kennedy Center for the Performing Arts in Washington, D.C., in 1989. She died in California in 1990, but she too came home to Texas: her cremated remains are buried in Weatherford. ★

Babe Didrikson Zaharias, Sports Heroine

Texas was home to one of the most remarkable women ever to enter the sports arena. To date, no one has equaled her performance in a variety of events, from track and field to golf. She set record after record, yet today remains largely unknown.

Babe Didrikson Zaharias was born Mildred Didriksen in Port Arthur, Texas, in 1914. She acquired the name "Babe," because of her batting talent in sandlot baseball—the boys she played with thought she hit like Babe Ruth. And she changed the spelling of her last name to emphasize that she was of Norwegian, not Swedish, descent.

After a hurricane nearly destroyed Port Arthur in 1915, the family moved to Beaumont, where Babe, her two brothers, and her sister grew up in a rough part of the city. She was a tomboy who wore her hair cut short like a boy, wore boyish clothing, and was constantly involved in fights. Babe was not popular in school, nor was she a good student. She usually just squeaked by to qualify for an athletic team.

In high school, she played volleyball, tennis, baseball, and basketball and was a swimmer. Basketball, which was popular at the time, was her best sport, and her high school team never lost a game while she was a member.

Didrikson dropped out of high school because Casualty Insurance Company in Dallas recruited her for their Golden Cyclone basketball team. She worked as a stenographer and led the company team to the national championship in 1933. In some games, she scored more than thirty points. She found herself more and more interested in track and field events and became a member of the Golden Cyclone track team, soon becoming the top performer in the country. In July 1932 she entered the national amateur track meet for women in Evanston, Illinois, as a single-member team and won the women's team championship. The second-place club had twenty members. Didrikson broke four world records that afternoon and gave a performance never before seen from a man or a woman in track-and-field history. That event led to a place on the US team in the 1932 Olympics in Los Angeles.

At the Olympics, she won two gold medals and a silver and set a world's record. The sports press loved her; her fellow competitors disliked her, calling her overbearing and aggressive.

At the end of the year she was named Woman Athlete of the Year by the Associated Press, a title she won five more times. But in 1932 the Amateur Athletics Union declared her a professional, ineligible for amateur events. She turned to exhibition basketball games, billiard matches, anything to make a living. In 1933 she organized Babe Didrikson's All-Americans, a women's basketball team, and toured small towns, challenging the local men's teams. In 1934 she pitched in major league spring training games and later played with a non-league team.

Golf was one of the few sports where women were accepted, and Didrikson was determined to learn to play. She took lessons and practiced until her hands were bloody. A year after her first tournament, she won the Texas Women's Amateur Championship. But once again, she was barred as an amateur because she had previously been a professional in sports. She toured the country in exhibition matches.

Babe Didrikson Zaharias. *Courtesy Dallas Public Library.*

In 1938 she married professional wrestler George Zaharias. During the war, she gave exhibition matches to raise money for war bonds. When she stayed away from professional play for three years, her amateur status was restored, and she became one of the most famous women golfers in history, winning tournament after tournament. She was the first American to win the British Women's Amateur. In 1947, she turned professional again and earned $100,000 in exhibitions and promotions, many times the amount she could win on the tournament circuit. She earned the most money of any woman golfer.

53

In 1953, Zaharias was diagnosed with colon cancer and underwent extensive surgery. Doctors said she'd never play again, but fourteen weeks later, she played in a tournament and went on to win the Ben Hogan Comeback of the Year Award, the United States Women's Open, and another Woman Athlete of the Year Award. By 1955 the cancer had returned, and doctors could do nothing. She died in Galveston in 1956.

Babe Didrikson Zaharias might reasonably be called the greatest woman athlete of all time. But she was also a force for equality, moving into athletic areas where women had not been before and refusing to follow the stereotypes of feminine behavior. As a result her sexuality was questioned, and she was even suspected of being a man in disguise (until she married Zaharias). Didrikson was courageous both in her professional life and her personal life, especially in the way she faced her final illness.

In 1955 Babe Zaharias established the Babe Zaharias Trophy to honor outstanding female athletes. ★

CULINARY ENTREPRENEURS

Women are traditionally associated with food. Long before feminism and the women's movement, Texas women brought a different flair to their cooking—and some of them made a business out of it.

NINNIE BAIRD

THERE WAS NINIA LILLA "Ninnie" Baird who, faced with supporting her family and invalid husband, developed a career as a baker and established a long-running and well known bakery. She had built a reputation for her bread and baked goods at the family restaurant before her husband's illness forced them to give it up.

Ninnie Baird developed a bread-baking business in her home. Her oldest son was her assistant baker, and her three younger sons delivered the bread. By 1918, she had established a bakery and was selling bread to grocery stores. Next came a bakery in Dallas and then a plant that was a landmark for many years in Fort Worth. Located at the corner of Summit and Lancaster avenues, the plant had glass windows so passersby could watch the bread-making—and it treated everyone in the area to the delicious aroma of fresh-baked bread.

By the 1950s Mrs Baird's Bakeries, with additional plants in Houston and Abilene, was the largest independent bakery operation in the United States. By 1961, when Ninnie Baird died, it operated nine plants. In 1998, a Mexican baking conglomerate purchased the business. ★

Ninnia Lilla Baird, *in her factory speaking with an unidentified man. Courtesy Mrs Baird's Bakeries.*

Lucille Bishop Smith *demonstrating her hot roll mix.*
Courtesy The Woman's Collection, Texas Woman's University.

LUCILLE BISHOP SMITH

LUCILLE BISHOP SMITH MADE her reputation with chili biscuits. When she taught vocational education in the Fort Worth public schools, she focused on domestic service training, which was considered appropriate for African-American women. She later moved on to Prairie View A&M College where she developed service training manuals. In 1941, she published *Lucille's Treasure Chest of Fine Foods*, a card file cookbook.

Her great success came when she developed a hot roll mix for busy housewives. She demonstrated her product at grocery stores and became the first African-American woman to join the Fort Worth Chamber of

Commerce. She continued to hold a variety of positions, but her greatest success was with chili biscuits—housewives could take those spicy morsels home, freeze them, bake them, and serve them as though they'd made them. Except everyone knew about Lucille and her chili biscuits. ★

HELEN CORBITT

To THIS DAY THE DOYENNE of Texas cooking is Helen Corbitt. She was to Texas cooking what Julia Child was to French cooking. Best known for directing food service in the Zodiac Room on the top floor of Dallas' Neiman Marcus store, she once protested that she had already established her reputation by the time Stanley Marcus lured her to Dallas.

Born in 1906 in upstate New York, she attended Skidmore College, intending to become a doctor. But her family lost everything in the Depression, and she put her home economics degree to work by serving as a therapeutic dietitian in hospitals. The work held no charm for her, and she was looking for a new position when the University of Texas at Austin offered her a position teaching quantity cooking classes and tea room management. She came to Austin in 1955.

Helen Corbitt hated Texas. When she moved to Houston to oversee food preparation at Joske's department

Helen Corbitt. *Courtesy Dallas Public Library.*

store, it took her six months to unpack her suitcase and a year to unpack her trunk. Asked to prepare a meal with Texas ingredients, she invented Texas caviar, that spicy dish based on black-eyed peas. From Joske's she went to the Houston Country Club and then to the Driskill Hotel in Austin, where she became friends with Lyndon Johnson and his family. LBJ wanted her to come to the White House, but she refused. Eventually, she called herself a "Texan by adoption."

Stanley Marcus courted her for eight years before she finally told him she was ready to come to Dallas. She presided over the Zodiac Room until 1969 when she retired to travel and lecture. During those years she also taught cooking classes in her home, the most famous being the "No Name Gourmet School for Men." She wrote several cookbooks: *Helen Corbitt's Cookbook, Helen Corbitt's Potluck, Helen Corbitt Cooks for Looks, Helen Corbitt Cooks for Company,* and *Helen Corbitt's*

59

Greenhouse Cookbook. She had by 1978 become interested in developing low-calorie menus for the Neiman Marcus spa, The Greenhouse. In the late 1960s, told that she must lose weight, she developed her own diet, according to the principles learned in her hospital dietitian days, and lost a dramatic amount of weight.

Still, if you want to cook frogs' legs or Lobster Thermidor or Beef au Poivre, Chantilly Cake or Strawberries Romanoff, Corbitt's cookbooks will tell you how to do it. In 2000 the University of North Texas Press published *The Best from Helen Corbitt's Kitchens,* edited by Patty Vineyard MacDonald.

Helen Corbitt insisted on the freshest fruit and vegetables, and she wanted the latter cooked al dente—no soggy, overcooked broccoli. Typical of her day, she made lots of molded salads, and she used butter and sour cream with abandon, though she usually recommended half and half instead of pure cream. She dispensed such tidbits as the fact that an odd number of shrimp on a plate looks better than an even number.

Helen Corbitt was a red-headed Irish woman with a temper to match. She had a sharp sense of humor and a strong personality. Independent, sassy, impatient, and a perfectionist, she brooked no interference. Even Stanley Marcus was not allowed in her kitchen without invitation. But throughout her life she developed a cadre of loyal friends and employees, because she cared about people. ★

POLITICS ON THE DISTAFF SIDE

GOVERNOR MIRIAM "MA" FERGUSON

IN 1924 TEXAS VOTED FOR Miriam "Ma" Ferguson and became the first state in the Union to elect a woman as governor. (Governor Nellie Ross of Wyoming, who took the governorship when her husband died, was inaugurated a few days before Governor Ferguson, so the crown of first woman governor rests lightly on each of their heads.)

Miriam Amanda Wallace was raised in a close family, sent to the best schools in Central Texas, and expected to marry a suitable man and raise a family. She wasn't much interested in men until Jim Ferguson, a neighbor and, by marriage, a distant relative, came along. He was everything she wasn't—big, loud, and uneducated, he had wandered the West working in restaurants, on railroads, even in gold mines. He was known for his temper and the wild stories he told about his life out West. And, while she was a devoted churchgoer, Jim was not.

For reasons known only to herself, she married Ferguson. They had two daughters, and he was a successful banker in Belton and Temple. When he announced he wanted to run for governor, she urged him to stick to banking where he was successful. But he persisted. He was elected but impeached in his second term; meantime, his banks failed, and his fortune was gone. In 1924, he decided that his wife should run for governor to redeem the family honor.

Miriam Ferguson never really wanted to be governor—she wanted to stay home, raise her daughters, and work in her garden. But she believed her husband knew best, and she followed his lead. A true cornball politician, he coined the names "Ma" and "Pa" during the

Miriam "Ma" Ferguson.
Courtesy Texas State Library and Archives Commission.

first campaign to emphasize that he and his wife were just plain folk. Miriam Ferguson's daughter said in reality no one would have dared call her mother "Ma." The Fergusons' campaign slogan was "Two governors for the price of one."

During his wife's term in office, ex-governor Ferguson had a desk right next to hers, and she deferred to him on many decisions. Miriam Ferguson served two terms as governor: from 1925–1927 and from 1933–1935. Her opponent in the second election, Ross Sterling, filed suit in court to keep her name off the ballot, charging that she won the primary with illegal votes. But Ma and Pa successfully hid from the process servers who would serve the official papers. Her name was on the ballot, and she won the election.

Historians have generally dismissed Miriam "Ma" Ferguson as one of the state's less important governors. She pardoned almost two thousand prisoners, either with full or conditional pardons. She opposed the Ku Klux Klan and prohibition (a teetotaler herself, she thought prohibition did not stop people from drinking and encouraged the illegal sales of alcohol). She was a fiscal conservative, and during the Depression found federal programs to help people who had lost their jobs. Because she loved horse races, she legalized betting at racetracks in Texas.

Jim Ferguson was a drag on her reputation—he was accused of taking bribes for criminal pardons, and he once persuaded his wife to appoint him to the Texas

State Highway Commission, where he awarded highway contracts for political reasons. People thought he was really running the state in the governor's place.

While in office, she entertained such celebrities as Will Rogers—he loved her chili—and after her second term, she traveled to Hollywood, where she was entertained like a star. In 1940 she ran for governor again and lost to Pappy O'Daniel (creator of the country music group, The Light-Crust Doughboys).

Although her daughters were now grown, Ferguson, then sixty-five, still wanted to stay in her Austin home and work in her garden, but she didn't think a Yankee should be governor of Texas (O'Daniel was originally from the North). She lost the election.

In spite of his shady political dealings, Miriam Ferguson loved her husband deeply. She was devastated when he died in 1944, and when she herself died in 1961, it was said the last words on her lips were, "Jim! Jim! Jim!"

Miriam Ferguson may have been one of the state's weakest governors, but she has become a folk heroine—and Texans are proud to have elected the first woman governor. ★

Barbara Jordan. *Courtesy Texas State Library and Archives Commission.*

BARBARA JORDAN

TEXAS WAS ALSO HOME to Barbara Jordan, the first black woman elected to the Texas state legislature, the first to serve as governor-for-a-day in any state, and the first elected to the United States House of Representatives from the South. Barbara Jordan also set a lot of other "firsts" for African-American women in the South.

Born in 1936 in Houston's Fourth Ward—a black community—Barbara Jordan always said several incidents in her life led her to challenge the existing social and political structure. In her senior year of high school, a black woman lawyer spoke at her school, and

Jordan knew what she wanted to do with her life. In college at Texas Southern University, an all-black school, she traveled with the debate team and proved that she could debate against Anglo girls—and win. But when the team traveled outside Houston, Jordan saw the reality of discrimination. The team often traveled for miles and miles without finding a restaurant or restroom they were allowed to use.

In 1962, with the encouragement of Democratic officials, she ran for the Texas House of Representatives, although she had to borrow the $500 filing fee. She had by then been to law school at Boston University—her first experience in an integrated world—and had practiced law in Houston, worked on the speakers' circuit for the campaigns of John F. Kennedy and Lyndon B. Johnson, and been active in PUSH—People for Upgrading Schools in Houston, the group that eventually forced the Houston school board to stop stalling and integrate the schools as ordered by the court some ten years earlier. When she was named assistant to Harris County Judge Bill Elliott, in 1965, she became the first black woman, other than cleaning women, to work in the courthouse.

Barbara Jordan lost that first election, although she drew out a heavier black vote than usual. In 1964, she ran again and lost again. In 1966, she ran for the state senate. If she lost, she said, it would be her last political race. She won 64 percent of the vote and was sworn in January 10, 1967. She found herself in a state senate that was all male, all white, mostly Democratic, mostly conservative, and mostly lawyers. Although she usually voted with Democrats, they could not assume she would do so—she was an independent thinker. Her first term was only two years, and in 1968 she ran again, unopposed.

In 1967 she served as governor-for-a-day and was appointed the first black vice-chair of the Texas Democratic Party. President Lyndon Johnson noticed her and called her to Washington for meetings. When she later announced a run for Congress, President Johnson was one of her major supporters and made a campaign appearance for her. The primary was a difficult battle, but she won. The November 1972 general election was not as difficult—Texas was then still a Democratic state. The national press carried stories about the first African-American woman from the South elected to the U.S. Congress.

She attended Harvard University's Congressional "Head Start" program where new members of Congress learn about their duties and the branches of government they will be working with. She worked hard at getting to know her fellow representatives and let them know her, and she was soon secretary of the Texas delegation and one of only three women in the Black Congressional Caucus. But once again, she proved herself independent and did not always do what the caucus wanted her to. Known for not socializing, she worked twelve- to fourteen-hour days and was always present for a vote.

In 1976 she shared keynote honors at the Democratic convention with former astronaut Senator John Glenn. In her speech, she talked of what it meant both to her and to the country that a black woman was given the honor of making that major address. During the Watergate scandal and the impeachment proceedings against President Richard Nixon, Jordan, a member of the Judiciary Committee, reviewed the case carefully. In 1974 she spoke on national television in favor of impeachment. Once again, she got national attention. The House voted for impeachment, but the president resigned before impeachment proceedings could be brought to the Senate.

While still in the House of Representatives, Jordan began to have health problems. She was diagnosed with multiple sclerosis, a chronic and progressive muscular disease. In her last term in Congress, Jordan pushed for an extension of the Voting Rights Act that would include Texas. She also worked for the Equal Rights Amendment. At the 1976 Democratic convention, she was one of several keynote speakers and her name was mentioned for vice president. But she knew that it was time, because of her illness, to leave national politics.

She went back to Texas, this time to Austin. In 1979, she began to teach at the University of Texas' Lyndon Baines Johnson School of Public Affairs. Although from that point on the public saw less of her in newspapers and television, she continued to be an active national voice. In 1994 she served on the U.S. Commission on Immigration Reform and received the Medal of Freedom, and in 1995 she delivered the Nancy Hanks Lecture on Arts and Public Policy. She was the seventy-seventh recipient of the Spingarn Medal for Enrichment of Afro-American Heritage from the National Association for the Advancement of Colored People.

Barbara Jordan never married, although she was always surrounded by many loyal friends. In her later years, she was confined to a wheelchair. She died in 1996 at the age of fifty-nine of complications from multiple sclerosis. At her funeral, President Clinton and Texas Governor Ann Richards celebrated her life. She was buried in the Texas State Cemetery, the first African American to be buried there.

Barbara Jordan once said, "I never intended to become a run-of-the-mill person." She wasn't. ★

ANN RICHARDS

ANN RICHARDS WAS the second woman governor of Texas, serving from 1991 to 1995. Unlike Miriam "Ma" Ferguson, Ann Richards ran on her own record of involvement with politics.

Richards grew up in a small Texas town during the Depression. She attended high school in Waco and went to Girls State, a program sponsored by the Women's Auxiliary of the American Legion in which students conduct a mock government in the state capitol for one week.

She attended Baylor University. By the time she graduated in 1954, she and David Richards were married. When he enrolled in law school at the University of Texas at Austin, she earned a teaching certificate and taught social studies and history in a junior high school.

David Richards opened a law practice in Dallas, and the couple raised four children. She had first become politically active at UT-Austin, and she remained so in Dallas, volunteering for the Democratic Party and helping found the North Dallas Democratic Women and the Dallas Committee for Peaceful Integration.

David Richards moved his family back to Austin, where she became involved with the Zoning and Planning Commission. Next she managed Sarah Weddington's successful 1972 campaign for the state legislature. Weddington, known for her law-changing abortion case before the Supreme Court, *Roe v. Wade,* became the first Austin woman elected to the Texas House of Representatives.

Ann Richards took her own step into politics in 1975. She ran for county commissioner, targeting voters who were likely to vote in small elections and sending them brightly-colored postcards, more likely to be read than letters. She defeated a man who had held the job for twelve years. As county commissioner, she supervised road crews. When she called her first meeting with

Ann Richards. *Courtesy Texas State Library and Archives Commission.*

them, she faced forty unfriendly men. They did not like reporting to a woman. She talked thirty minutes, telling stories, asking about their families—nothing changed their expressions. One of the men had an extremely ugly dog, and finally she asked the dog's name.

"Ann Richards," answered the man. The men waited—but she laughed aloud, and then they laughed. Now her friends, they renamed the dog Miz Richards.

In 1977, President Jimmy Carter appointed her to the Advisory Committee on Women. In Texas, she helped organize a traveling exhibit called "Women in Texas." She also helped organize Leadership Texas, a program designed to introduce promising female leaders to various aspects of life in the state.

In the early 1980s, Richards successfully ran for state treasurer and began for the first time to be active on the national political scene. She campaigned for Geraldine Ferraro as vice president in 1984 and for Michael Dukakis in his unsuccessful 1988 try for the presidency. That year she gained national attention when she was the keynote speaker at the National Democratic Convention. Richards, who later confessed to nervousness, drew laughs when she drawled in her Texas accent, "Poor George! He was born with a silver foot in his mouth." George Bush, Sr., the Republican candidate, was known for misspeaking.

Ann Richards decided to run for governor of Texas in the 1990 election because she thought she could bring needed change to the state, and she thought she could win. She ran against billionaire rancher and oilman Clayton Williams, Jr., who had no experience in politics or government but had a lot of money to finance his campaign. Williams lost the election with one gesture: when Richards reached to shake his hand, he did not offer his own hand, as a gentleman should.

Richards won and immediately established a style for her term in office. She was having fun. She became known for her silver-white "big hair" and for riding a motorcycle. Her speech was colorful. Once, wanting to convince lawmen that a problem was already upon them and not to be forestalled, she said, "Gentlemen, the ox is in the ditch." Another time she served legislators cornbread and coffee in the mansion while she talked to them about a school finance bill.

Ann Richards proudly pointed out that when she was elected, Texas was $6 billion in debt. When she left office, there was a $2 billion surplus. She attracted over seven thousand new jobs to Texas. When she came into office, the state was in federal court because its schools, mental health institutions, and prisons did not meet federal standards. When she left, those institutions were up to standard. She defeated a concealed handgun law (later passed by the Bush administration), made midnight raids on nursing homes, lobbied for fair insurance laws, and created a lottery to help the state's budget.

But her most important accomplishment was to open government to women and minorities. She appointed three times as many Latinos and five times as many African Americans to positions of responsibility than any previous governor, setting, she hoped, a pattern for all governors in all states.

Richards ran for re-election in 1994 but was defeated by George W. Bush. She died of cancer in 2007. ★

Molly Ivins. *Courtesy of* Texas Observer.

MOLLY IVINS

MOLLY IVINS CAME AT POLITICS from a different angle. She was a political columnist, commentator, and author, and in Texas, she was a legend.

Ivins began her career in the complaint department of the *Houston Chronicle* and went on to be a city reporter. Moving from Texas to Minneapolis, she was the first woman police reporter on the *Minneapolis Tribune* staff and later covered movements for social change, which brought her into contact with militant blacks and Indians, radical students, and others.

In 1970 she headed home to Texas and from then until 1976 wrote for *The Texas Observer*, a liberal Austin bi-

74

weekly. Next she wrote for *The New York Times* from 1976 until 1982, including a stint as Rocky Mountain bureau chief, a title she claimed she got because there was no one else in the bureau. Her colorful, colloquial style frequently put her in hot water with the top editors. In 1982, she went to the *Dallas Times Herald*, where she stayed until the paper folded in 1992. The *Fort Worth Star-Telegram* was her home paper until 2001, when she became a syndicated columnist and independent journalist.

In all her writing, Ivins was outspoken and irreverent. She called President George W. Bush "Shrub" and Texas Governor Rick Perry "Mr. Good Hair."

Ivins authored or co-authored several books, including *Bushwhacked: Life in George W. Bush's America* (with Lou Dubose, 2003), *The Betrayal of America: How the Supreme Court Undermined the Constitution and Chose Our President* (with Vincent Bugliosi, 2001), *Shrub: The Short But Happy Political Life of George W. Bush* (with Lou DuBose, 2000), *Molly Ivins Can't Say That, Can She?* (1991), and others.

Her awards include the William Allen White Award from the University of Kansas, the Smith Medal from Smith College, the Pringle Prize for Washington Journalism from Columbia University, the Eugene V. Debs Award in journalism, and many others. Friends say she used the awards as trivets on the dining table at dinner parties. She said, however, that the two awards she was most proud of were the naming of the Minneapolis Police

Department mascot pig after her and her banishment from speaking on the Texas A&M University Campus while she was with *The Texas Observer*.

Molly Ivins was diagnosed with breast cancer in 1999; it returned in 2003 and again in 2005. She died in January 2007. In one of her last published columns, she urged readers to "keep fightin' for freedom and justice, beloveds, but don't you forget to have fun doin' it. Lord, let your laughter ring forth. Be outrageous, ridicule the fraidy-cats, rejoice in all the oddities that freedom can produce. And when you get through kickin' ass and celebratin' the sheer joy of a good fight, be sure to tell those who come after how much fun it was."

In a loving tribute to Molly Ivins, *The Texas Observer* wrote, "Molly was a hero. She was a mentor. She was a liberal. She was a patriot. She was a friend. And she will always be with us." ★

LADYBIRD JOHNSON

When Texans hear the name Ladybird Johnson, they think of the fields of bluebonnets and Indian paintbrush that line our highways. But Ladybird was much more than a lady who wanted to beautify America. She was a wife, mother, politician in her own right, businesswoman, and conservation advocate. She once said she would be remembered only as Lyndon Baines

Ladybird Johnson. *Courtesy Ladybird Johnson Wildflower Center*

Johnson's wife, but by the time of her death in 2007, history had already proved otherwise.

Born Claudia Alta Taylor in 1912 in Karnack, a small town in East Texas, she was immediately called Ladybird by a nursemaid. The name stuck—in spite of her determined attempts to shed it. Her mother died when she was six, and her father, a dynamic businessman, was engaged with his cotton gins, real estate, and general store much of the time. Her siblings were much older, and young Ladybird spent time alone, often wandering in the woods of East Texas. There, she said, she developed her love of the outdoors, and all her life she would put off going indoors as long as she could.

After high school graduation at the age of fifteen—too young, she later said—she went to boarding school in Dallas and then enrolled in the University of Texas at Austin. When she received the BA, she enrolled for a second degree in journalism. In the fall of 1934, when she was twenty-one, she met Lyndon Johnson. Later, she recalled, "I knew that I had met something remarkable, but I didn't quite know what." Johnson proposed on their first date, which somewhat alarmed her, but she kept seeing him. They were married in November, two-and-a-half months after meeting.

Ladybird, always shy, learned to be outgoing as her husband rose in political importance. Her inherent southern graciousness often came to her rescue. She entertained for him, met all the social obligations, took a public speaking course, and followed his gentle urgings to be more outgoing and spruce up her appearance. When Johnson served in the U. S. Navy in World War II, she ran his congressional office. Later, she bought a radio station in Austin and nurtured it to success and growth. Every week, in Washington, D.C., she received a thick packet of papers, reporting on activities at the station.

The Johnsons were married ten years before the birth of their daughter, Lynda Bird, in 1944. Luci Baines, arrived in 1947, and in 1948, her husband ran for the Senate. Ladybird campaigned actively, something most wives did not do in those days. In 1960, when her husband ran for the Democratic presidential nomination, she campaigned again. The nomination went to John F. Kennedy, who asked Johnson to be his vice-presidential candidate. Johnson wanted to refuse, but Ladybird said, "Power is where power goes." Once again, she campaigned for the ticket, because Jacqueline Kennedy, expecting her third child, could not actively campaign. The ticket was elected.

Of her husband's painful elevation to president after the assassination of President Kennedy, Ladybird said, "I feel I was thrust on the stage for a role I never had the chance to rehearse." But she had been the wife of a congressional aide, a congressman, a senator, and the vice president. She rose gracefully to the occasion. She was occasionally criticized for being a country hick with a southern drawl. Once she told a crowd in the South, "You may not agree with what I have to say, but at least you will understand the way I say it."

The presidential years were difficult for the Johnsons. The successes of the Great Society were lost in the furor over the Vietnam War and the national protests against that war. A bright spot for Ladybird was the passage of the 1965 Highway Beautification Bill, known as Ladybird's Bill. Working actively to see the bill through Congress, Ladybird moved into the political arena in a way that no First Lady had before her. Some criticized her for stepping out of her role as First Lady. Others charged that she concentrated on something unimportant when the nation was at war. She was undaunted by the criticism. And if today's highways are relatively free of billboards and junkyards, it is because of Ladybird and "her" bill.

During the presidency, Ladybird once said, "Lyndon lives in a cloud of trouble." She supported his decision not to run for a second term of his own—he had finished Kennedy's term and served one term on his own—and added the phrase "and shall not accept" to the speech in which he announced, "I shall not seek my party's nomination." In January 1969, the Johnsons retired to their beloved ranch on the Pedernales River in the Texas Hill Country. President Johnson died in 1973, after a series of heart attacks.

After a period of ill health following Johnson's death, Ladybird resumed public activity, raising funds for the LBJ Museum, serving on the University of Texas Board of Regents, continuing her beautification work. In 1982 she donated money to establish the National Wildflower Research Center, since renamed the Ladybird Johnson Wildflower Center. She maintained her home at the ranch and a home in Austin, where her daughters and their families lived.

Ladybird suffered a stroke in 2002, which left her unable to speak. Still she made public appearances and maintained an active, if limited, schedule. She died in 2007 at the age of ninety-four, and all of Texas—and the nation—mourned.

Lyndon Johnson could be charming and genial, and he could be loud and offensive, but there has never been any controversy about Ladybird. Former Speaker of the House Jim Wright said, "I don't believe I ever heard her say anything disparaging about anyone. I've known a lot of people on the other side politically from Lyndon who had dislike for him, but I never have known anyone who had a dislike for Ladybird." ★

BOOKS TO EXPLORE

Alter, Judy. *Extraordinary Women of the American West.*
Danbury, CT: Children's Press, 2000. Written for
5th graders but still a source of basic information.

_____. *Henrietta King, Rancher and Philanthropist.* Abilene:
State House Press, 2005. Written for 4th graders but
gives a basic outline of her life.

_____. *Miriam "Ma" Ferguson, First Woman Governor of Texas.*
Abiline: State House Press, 2006. Also written for
4th graders.

Crawford, Ann Fears, and Crystal Sasse Ragsdale. *Women
in Texas: Their Lives, Their Experiences, Their
Accomplishments.* Abilene: State House Press, 1992.

Hunt, Annie Mae, Ruthe Winegarten, and Frieda Warden. *I
Am Annie Mae: An Extraordinary Black Woman in
Her Own Words.* Austin: University of Texas Press,
1996.

Massey, Sara R. *Texas Women on the Cattle Trails.* College
Station: Texas A&M University Press, 2006.

Notable American Women: A Biographical Dictionary. (4 vols.).
Cambridge, MA: Harvard University Press, 1971-
1980.

Roach, Joyce. *The Cowgirls.* Denton: University of North Texas
Press, 1990.

Winegarten, Ruthe. *Black Texas Women: A Sourcebook.* Austin:
University of Texas Press, 1996.

ABOUT THE AUTHOR

JUDY ALTER is the author of numerous books, fiction and nonfiction, for adults and young adults. She has a particular interest in the lives of women in Texas and the American West. She lives in Fort Worth. ★

Extraordinary Texas Women
ISBN 978-0-87565-366-2
Case. $8.95
A Texas Small Book

ISBN 978-0-87565-366-2

9 780875 653662

5 0 8 9 5